The Gift
by the Pond

KAREN SWASEY

Edited by Lil Barcaski

Published by: GWN Publishing
www.GWNPublishing.com

Cover Design: Kristina Conatser

Paperback ISBN: 978-1-965971-02-4

Hardcover ISBN: 978-1-965971-03-1

DEDICATION

To the dreamers and believers in the magic of kindness, this book is dedicated to you. May each page remind you that a single act of kindness can create a ripple effect, spreading warmth, positivity, and endless possibilities to someone's life.

Let the words within inspire you to perform small acts of kindness, pursue your passions, and ignite change in the world.

SOMEWHERE IN TIME...

We all have a place where we remember the gift of a lifetime given to us from another person in our life. This person may have been a stranger, or a friend, but this gift they gave you has stayed with you through your entire life. Such a gift as this has happened to me, and here is my story...

In a small town in Maine, as a little girl, I grew up surrounded by adventures and imaginary friends. My friends and I would explore the forests during the summers and skate on the ponds in the winters, enjoying every moment to our hearts' content.

One of these ponds was located right in the middle of our small town, just down from the schoolyard where we would play after school. It had stumps and alders poking up from the ice, creating perfect spots for playing tag as we darted in and out of the bushes. At night, we would gather around bonfires built by our brothers, warming ourselves and sharing stories of the adventures we had yet to explore. It was a time of joy and the anticipation of stories yet to come.

To reach the pond from the school, you had to go by a path that led to a shack deep in the woods. The shack was a short distance from the pond, situated at the base of the hill. Although you couldn't see it from the pond itself, we would always try to catch a glimpse of it through the alders while skating. There was a man who lived in that shack, and we kids were always afraid of him. He never spoke to us when we saw him on the sidewalk, and he had only one arm, with his green work shirt sleeve pinned up to his shoulder.

This man always wore a green hat that matched his shirt and pants. The hat was always tilted to one side of his head, frayed on the edges, and a little dirty on the bill. He was an old man with a weathered face and only one large hand. I would watch him pass my house on his way to sit on his stool at the local grocery store and lunch counter.

I would sit in the window and watch him pass by the house wondering what ever happened to his arm and why I never saw him smile. I would imagine what might have happened for him to lose his arm and if he ever had a family...curious as a child, I would create all kinds of imaginary stories.

As kids, we would imagine what his shack would look like and thought it must be like a hobbit house (as no one had ever made it down the path to see the shack itself) and we would talk back and fourth to what it might look like inside. We would dare each other to go all the way down the path to peek at the shack and then

tell tales of how we went and looked into the windows and saw what was inside. Each child out doing the other with this imaginary tale of how they risked life and limb going down the path and not getting caught.

One day we all gathered at the top of the hill at the beginning of the path that lead to the shack. There we were, five kids daring each other to go down into the dark path to the hobbit house by the edge of the pond into the deep dark forest. And then it happened, it was my turn to take the "walk" into the forest.

Trying to brave and taking a deep breath, I turned to my friends and said, "I'm not afraid, I'm going all the way down to the shack, you just wait and see."

I had no idea what lied ahead on this dark trail before me and I imagined it being a stairway made out of rock steps leading to a deep dark place into the forest.

The path was lined with high blueberry bushes that stretched onto the path and brushed up against me as I walked down the dark path. I felt I had gone further than the others as no one had ever mentioned that the pond that we skated on actually came close to the paths edge, so I decided to go around the next bend in the path as it figured it couldn't be too much further to get to the shack.

I kept on thinking about my friends being at the top of the hill wondering if I am just hiding behind a pine tree counting to one hundred, staying down on the trail long enough to look like I made it there. Betty and Iris would never believe I had made it this far as it was, and Butch and Glen would be betting wether or not I even made it to the old fallen tree in the bend. But I really had to get there this time as people would just say I was telling a tall tale again.

Little did I know, but my brother showed up and was asking my friends what we were up to standing at the top of the path looking like there was some mischief going on. And he said, "By the way...where was Karen?"

With each step I just had to say to myself, just keep going. As I walked, I intensely listened to the rustle of leaves under my feet and then jumping out of my skin every time I heard a squirrel scurrying in the trees; my heart was pounding like a freight train was coming and I could hardly breathe!

As I came around the bend, there in the grove of tall pine and fir trees was this small cabin. Huh..it wasn't a hobbit house after all. It had a porch to sit on and a stove pipe that came out of the roof. The roof was covered with pine needles and it had small framed windows on either side of the front door. As I stood there I thought, this isn't as scary of a place as I thought it would be, it is actually a very cute cabin.

The old cabin nestled next to the pond

My thoughts were overshadowed by how hard my heart was pounding. I wasn't sure if the man could see me from inside the cabin, so I crouched down behind the blueberry bushes on the path. My mind was racing, thinking about how excited I will be telling my friends that the cabin is really close to where we skate. The man from the cabin was probably watching us peeking at him through the alder bushes. I had better go tell them quickly!

So I took one last look and twirled around to scurry back up the path as fast as I could go. As I was running past the pond area by the path, I took one last look

over the blueberry bushes to see if I could recognize where on the pond this path was located... and then I turned around in fright!

There in front of me was the man who lived in cabin standing in the shadows of the path. I stood in full fright and gasped in my surprise.He just stood there looking at me and didn't say a word.

And I said, "I'm sorry sir, I promise I didn't touch anything. I just wanted to see the shack where you lived."

Oh no! What was going to happen to me!! I thought to myself.

As I stood there looking up at this weathered face of a man that was staring down at me, I felt myself trembling in my little white sneakers as my pigtails danced across my chest from my heart beating so hard. I was wondering what he was going to say or do to me.... then something absolutely amazing happened. The man with the green hat tipped on top of his head scooched down...and then he smiled.

All of a sudden, I wasn't as afraid as I was coming around that corner and seeing him in the shadows. His smile was a smile of kindness that I had never seen before. I am sure that my jaw dropped as I looked up at him with my big brown eyes thinking, *who is this man smiling down at me?*

The man in the tipped green hat stood back up and then stood off to the side of the path, pulled back the

blueberry bush so that I could scoot by him, and I ran back up to the top of the hill.

I could hardly wait to get to the top of the hill so that I could tell my friends that I actually made it to the shack. And then I could tell them that the shack wasn't actually a shack, but a cute little cabin, and that I actually ran into the man with one arm in the green tipped hat on the way back up the path.

I knew they must be waiting gazing down that long dark path thinking that the old man must of been in his cabin and I bet they thought he even captured me as it was taking so long for me to come back to tell them what I saw.

As I came to the top of the path, none of my friends were to be found. *Huh...* I stood there looking left and

then right to see if they were hiding amongst the bushes, but I couldn't find them anywhere.

Maybe they saw the man coming from down the road to go home to his cabin and they ran away so they wouldn't be caught, but...why wouldn't they have waited for me?

Oh! Wait!! I can hear voices down by the pond, maybe they ran down there to wait for me!!

I ran down to the pond to see if they were hiding down there, but there were only a bunch of kids playing in the pond catching frogs for the annual frog jumping contest that was in a couple of days.

I yelled out to Kenny, "Hey Kenny, have you seen Betty and Iris?"

"Naw, they haven't been here with us, come catch some frogs with us!"

I didn't have time for that right now as I needed to find my friends. I yelled, "Maybe later!" and I turned around and ran back up the trail to the road.

I kept running all the way back to my house to see if my friends were actually waiting for me there, as they knew that I was on that path going to the shack, but to my surprise, they weren't at my house either. So I ran across the street to Betty's house, and there they were, all gathered outside on the front steps eating popsicles.

I was completely out of breath when I ran up to the steps, and I hardly could speak to tell them what just happened to me. I babbled out, "Oh my goodness, I actually met the man on the path and saw his shack all the way at the bottom of the trail!"

They all looked at each other and laughed out loud saying, "Oh sure Karen, you never made it down there, you are just making this all up!" Laughing so hard at me.

*The old main street dirt road in the center
of Andover village*

*The old Andover town Library that
was originally a church from 1899*

I said, "Betty, Iris, you must believe me, I really saw him, and I really did get to the shack. It really wasn't that far beyond that bend in the path we made it to the other day."

They all were rolling with laugher. I stood there so upset that they didn't believe me. I took a deep breath and hung my head, turned around and walked home.

But while walking away, I kept thinking about the man's smile, and how I wasn't as afraid anymore of the man with the one arm and a green tipped hat. Something had changed in me. I knew I couldn't tell my mom that I was down there, so I just had to keep the gift to myself. I kept thinking, with a smile like that, I wondered what happened to him and how come he never spoke to us kids, and I wondered, why did he lived alone in that cute little cabin on the edge of pond? What must of happened in his life to hide such a nice smile?

When I went to bed that night, I had dreams from the discussions that I heard my parents have earlier that day. They talked about the old library in Andover that was just across from the path where this old man lived. They talked about how at one point in time it was a church, and I dreamed: *I wonder if this man was actually old enough to have gone to that church when it was a church and not a library.*

And then I went on to dream about the story that my parents was talking about at the kitchen table when Andover had a dirt road going down to the center of town, and there was a big hotel that people would come and stay at from around the world, and they would drive down to see the old covered bridge at the edge of town. And I dreamt:

Did this old man with one arm and a green tipped hat see this hotel, and did he have fun jumping from the windows of the old covered bridge as we did as kids.

The Lovejoy Covered Bridge built in 1867

THE NEXT DAY...

I was heading over to the frog pond to meet Kenny, who was going to help me catch a frog for the frog jumping contest that was going to be held in the town ball field for Old Home Days. When he didn't show up, I decided to go to his house to see if he had forgotten about helping me catch my frog.

When I arrived at his house, his brother was sitting on the stoop, working on a fishing line for his fishing pole. I walked up to him and said, "Hey Phil, is your brother home?"

You could tell he was annoyed as he was trying to thread the line through the loops on the fishing pole, and he said without looking at me, "He is at that old car you all play on in the field down by the pond."

I said, "Oh, thanks, sorry to bother you!"

He said, "Yup, no worries," and went back to his pole.

I turned on my heels and ran to the field by the pond near Betty's house, which is different from where the old man with the one arm and the green-tipped hat lived.

When I arrived, there were three boys playing, pretending they were traveling to Bethel and got stuck on the road as if they were driving the old car themselves. This old car behind Betty's house had been there so long that it had grown right into the ground.

The old car behind Betty's house
that we played in
pretending we traveled the world!

I hollered at Kenny, "Did you forget that you were going to meet me at the pond where we skate and catch a frog for the contest?"

He said, "Oh, I already caught you one for Sunday, and it is with the others for the jumping contest. Sorry I didn't let you know. Do you want to go to Bethel with us?"

I looked at the other two boys and could see they were not impressed at the thought of a girl joining them, so I said, "No, that's okay, you go ahead," playing along with their adventure.

Then Johnny from the back seat held up an old doll and shouted, "Hey, is this one of you girls' dolls? It sure is dirty."

"No, it isn't mine," I replied. I had not seen that doll there before.

He said, "I went to pull up the cushion, and it was tucked in between the seats. Okay, never mind." Then he threw it into the woods.

I thought to myself, *I couldn't let that doll just be thrown into the woods like that. What if it is someone's special doll?*

I am sure it has a story behind why it is there. So, I ran over, picked it up, and brushed off her dress.

Smiling at her as I walked away, for some reason, I thought, *Did the man with one arm and the green-tipped hat have a family at one point in time? Is that why he looked down at me and smiled, thinking of his little girl? Could this have been his car at one time?*

I am going to take this doll home, clean her up, and maybe one day I will be brave enough to ask him if this was his car and if this doll belonged to his little girl.

I thought of all the times I crawled into that back seat and never saw that doll there. Betty, Iris, and I used to take turns crawling behind the wheel of that old car, pretending we were traveling down an old tote road to see where the lumberjacks went after leaving my house in the wee hours of the morning.

You see, my mother ran a boarding home for the loggers in town. They would stay in the rooms up stairs in our house and mom would get up really early in the morning and bake muffins, make coffee and fry up bacon and eggs for the men before they went off to work in the woods.

I remember laying there in bed smelling the coffee and bacon waiting until it was time from me to go down to the kitchen. Sometimes I went down a little too early and I would see all the brown paper bags full of sandwiches, pickles and cookies that mom had made up for them on the counter waiting for them to grab on their way out the door. They all would turn and give me a little wave as they headed out the door, but I didn't remember if one of them was the man with one arm and the green tipped hat, I couldn't see their faces and I think I would have remembered him if he was staying there. Oh well, what is important now is that I am to take care of this doll.

Next weekend is the frog jumping contest after church on Sunday afternoon. Everyone in town will be there for this family fun event. People will be cheering and betting on which frog is going to win. I went over to Kenny's house, and he showed me my frog.

Boy, it was big! I'm sure to win with that one!

On that Sunday before the contest, I went to church all dressed up in my pretty black shoes and the blue dress that my mom bought just for Sundays like this. You see, this was a special Sunday because my friend's little baby sister was going to be baptized, and a lot of friends and family were going to be there.

The church was packed, and I saw the little baby have her head sprinkled with holy water as the pastor said a prayer. I was surprised she never even cried but looked up at her parents, almost smiling. The entire church gave an "Awwww" as we watched the ceremony.

After that part of the service, all the children went up to the belfry by the big old pipe organ, and we sang songs that we learned in Bible school, which the kids attend after the first part of the service. I stood there and waved to my mom as she peeked around the lady in front of her. I think we all did well, as everyone was smiling when we finished. This was a Sunday tradition in our town.

After church, all the townsfolk would gather to enjoy coffee and baked goods while the kids played around the common in the center of town.

But why did I never see my new friend, the man with one arm and a green- tipped hat?

When I got up the next day I started to reflect upon some of the things I looked forward to in our little town. Back in the 1960's in this small town in Maine, everyone took care of the children in the town. It was like having a great big family, but your were't related. If I wanted to talk to someone on the phone, I would simply pick up the phone and say to the operator, "Can I talk with Cam please?"

The operator would say, "Well you will have to wait a little while as she just walked into Hod's Store."

So there it is; life was simple, and everyone helped each other out as best they could and a safety net was there watching over the children.

Oh, and then there were Wednesday's....*oh my how I loved Wednesday's!!*

This was an absolute favorite day of mine as I would go over to our neighbors house and stand outside their window peeking through the window panes to see if Cam was making her very special spaghetti sauce.

You see, this lady Cam was Italian, and she and her husband would keep a tradition of their parents alive every Wednesday, it became "pasta day"!!

Oh how I loved pasta day!!

Cam would look out the window and give a little giggle and wave me in so I could enjoy a plate of her famous pasta.

When I went into the house to see Cam while she was fixing our pasta dinner, I thought about how I could share with her my encounter with the man with one arm in the green-tipped hat.

You see, Cam was my secret keeper; she was like a second mom to me. Sometimes you just need that special person to whom you can whisper your thoughts and know they are kept in a secret box.

As we set the table for our wonderful pasta dinner, I sat down and helped her fold the napkins.

I said, "Cam, do you know what happened to the man with one arm and the green-tipped hat who walks around town and doesn't talk to anyone? Do you know he lives down that path by the school, all the way down by the pond?"

She looked at me, sat down in the chair beside me, and said, "What makes you ask, my dear?"

"Well, the other day I did something that I'm not supposed to do, but I ended up making a friend, I think. When I walked down to sneak a peek at the cabin by the edge of the pond where the old man with one arm and the green-tipped hat lives, I turned around and he was standing right there behind me.

At first, I was really, really scared, but then something magical happened. He scooched down and smiled at me. And when he smiled at me, he no longer looked scary to me anymore. What happened to this smile that disappeared on this man with the one arm in the green-tipped hat?"

Cam went on to tell me that he was a very hard-working lumberjack. He and his family lived in town, and he had a wife who was about to have a baby. But one tragic day, while working in the lumberyard, he had an accident and lost his arm.

On that same sad day, his wife was traveling to the hospital with a friend and the roads were really slippery and they went off the road and sadly she and the baby passed away. Since then, this gentleman has been very sad.

Ever since that tragic event, he has lived at the end of that path, escaping from the world and all that has happened to him.

I started to think about all the thoughts I had, and they truly were a glimpse into his life that I didn't realize I could see. Deep within my heart, I could sense the pain this man was enduring.

Perhaps, just perhaps, when I went down to his cabin and looked up at him, apologizing for spying on him the way I did, he saw the gentle heart of a child. Maybe that's what made him smile. My mom always says, "We never know what little key will open a door for someone in their life."

Perhaps I was the one who held that key, just as my mom always says, to help him see the gift he is in life. Cam and I went on to finish setting the table, and they started to get the sauce and the fresh, warm bread ready to put down for our wonderful Wednesday Pasta Day meal.

Cam's pasta looked a little different than what my mom made, as it was this tube looking noodle Cam called a Roni. I would take my thumb and put it through the noodle and hold it up in the air admiring my success and pop it into my mouth all covered with sauce. There was plenty of evidence when I went home as I brought a good deal of it back on my shirt, but mom never minded, she knew exactly where I was on a Wednesday night for supper.

We had plenty of family traditions that I learned from as a child growing up in my little town in Maine. Betty's family was French Canadian and Armenian, and boy, could her mom make the most amazing breads! My mom, she made the best tasting scrapple from pork and cornmeal, which was poured into bread pans lined with wax paper. I remember we always had it when my gramps would come to stay with us, as it was his favorite food. I can still smell it cooking in the frying pan, and then Mom would pour fresh maple syrup from our neighbor's maple trees all over it. Mom was Scottish and German, and this was her tradition passed down through generations.

Iris's family had a tradition of a meat pie. It was from a French Canadian recipe that was her grandmothers. It was a little spicy with hamburg, ground pork, peppers and onions with small cut up potatoes in it. I kinda liked it anyway, especially the flaky crust!

All these thoughts kept rolling through my head, and I would wonder, *did the man with one arm and the green-tipped had have thoughts like mine? Did he have family traditions too?*

And then I would see that smile on his face again in my minds eye, and I would sigh; boy... he really did have such a kind face. I'm so glad mom told me about the key.

The next day I met up with Betty and Iris and we were hanging around outside at my house. We were laying on the lawn looking up at the big puffy clouds trying to see if we could make them into animals, when my mom came out the door and asked me to go down to the store and pick up her groceries. So Betty, Iris and I got up from the lawn and walked down to the store.

On the way there, we ran into Butch and Glen as they were riding their bikes to get a soda at the old soda fountain shop. We stopped and gathered out in front of the store and they started to tease me again about making it to the cabin.

I said to them, "You wait, one day you will see that I am telling the truth." And I walked inside to pick up the groceries that my mother had ordered. And guess what, there on a stool at the food counter to my left was the old man with the one arm in the green tipped hat. I stood there for a moment wondering, should I go over and say something to him?

Would this proved to my friends that I actually saw the man with the green tipped hat? *Do I dare?* And then I thought back to that smile. I turned to him as he slowly turned on the stool to look at me. I looked back at my friends to make sure they were watching me, and I picked up the bag of groceries off the counter, and took a few steps towards the old man with the one arm.

And guessed what happened? The old man with the green tipped hat looked at me and said, "Good morning young lady."

I stood there as proud as a peacock and said. "Good morning sir." I turned and tossed my chin to my friends and walked past them with the bag of groceries in my arms,

thinking to myself, *See, I do know the man who lives in the shack at the bottom of the hill by the pond.*

My friends all stood there with jaws dropped as I walked out the door. That day I smiled...all the way home.

Throughout my life, I have always remembered his kind smile and gentle nature. During my childhood years, he would stop by my house to say hello. He even befriended some of the local boys in town, who would visit his cabin and go fishing with him from time to time. He was even a judge for the frog jumping contest some years.

From the moment he shared his smile with me, he was no longer the scary man with only one arm; his life and ours changed in town. I often thought about the way he lost his arm in that lumber yard accident and how hard it must have been for him to adjust to life without an arm. I would think about his family from time to time.

I remember the day I went to his cabin by the pond and brought that old doll I found in the old car in the field. He held it and a tear came down his cheek.

I asked, "Is that your car in the field that we play in by Betty's house?"

He said, "Yes, the day after I came home from the hospital, I drove it down to the spot where my wife and I used to watch the deer drink from the pond and I parked it there. It has been there ever since. This was the doll I had bought for my yet-to-be-born little girl. Thank you for bringing her back to me," he said, and smiled with a golden tear on his cheek. That doll was a healing key to his life too.

Just like mom said, "We never know what the good Lord will use to heal a broken heart."

His life was a story, and the lessons he taught me are ones I still carry with me today. He has been an important part of my journey. Viewing life through the lens of others' experiences has been a gift he gave me.

As children, we possess vivid imaginations and a strong desire to explore the unknown. Howev-

er, it's important to pause and consider what might have inspired these imaginary stories. By looking beyond our first impressions, we can appreciate the gift of a well-lived life. The walk I took down that path that day profoundly changed my view of this man's life; and that all started with a smile.

No longer did he live in a shack that had grass on the roof and a hobbit door, but an adorable cabin that was in amongst the forest as a place of tranquility. This little piece of the planet was his sanctuary in life. Thinking back now, I see how the cabin was carefully maintained and how he must've enjoyed stepping out his door in the middle of the winter as he listened to the children laugh and play on the ice as they chased each other around through alder bushes playing tag.

We never truly know the gift of an encounter until we walk through different stages in our life. This encounter of the man with the green tipped hat on top of his head and a sleeve pinned to his shoulder from an arm that wasn't there, taught me to look beyond what I see at first glance. To look within someone who may have been burdened by pain, and see the person within, and honor their life story. To take the time to stop and to get to know someone without judging them by first impressions.

There are many gifts waiting for us on the stepping stones of life, and it is up to each of us to show kindness to those who may be hurting.

Maybe one day you too will find that *Gift by the Pond* as this man was to me, and cherish the friendship you received by looking beyond the green tipped hat worn by the man with one arm, who lived in the cabin by the pond. Look beyond the first impression and take the time to love one another, and you will find that your life will change forever as mine did too.

"Remember...If you judge people,
you have no time to love them."

A *Gift* from Mother Teresa for
all of us to follow

Now, this old man with the tipped hat upon his head walks hand-in-hand with his daughter, bringing to her the little doll he had bought for her years ago. No longer with only one arm, he is now whole, walking the path in heaven with his little girl forever more.

"The Artistry in this book was created by Karen Swasey...using her words to describe her thoughts and she created these images."

As a person with limitations resulting from an incident involving an ear of corn (yes, you read that right—an ear of corn, but that's a story for another day), I have a torn muscle behind my ear that has shifted into the collarbone area near my neck. This affects the circulation in my arm, so I must be careful not to overdo it when typing or lifting. Despite these challenges, I have found a unique way to express my thoughts through AI design.

These images were created by me, translating my thoughts into visuals to bring the book to life. Don't let limitations hold you back from possibilities and dreams; there are countless unique ways people have created ways to help individuals like me achieve their dreams. I hope you enjoyed these pictures as much as I enjoyed creating them! They are a vision from my mind, transformed from words into images for you to see. Never stop dreaming of possibilities...as said in the words of Rosa Montero:

"You'd be amazed at the infinite possibilities of the impossible."

www.ingramcontent.com/pod-product-compliance
Lightning Source LLC
Chambersburg PA
CBHW051247120626
46547CB00014B/1835